The
Passion Project

Your Quick and Practical Guide to Finding
Fulfillment in Life

Lynn Sheets

To Kevin, Bayla, & Kaia,

for showing me meaning and fulfillment.

CONTENTS

PREFACE

As I perused "top books on passion," I read descriptions about grit, looking on the bright side, how to make a buck, and a host of general advice such as: You can do anything. Just try it. The sky is the limit.[1]

No book seemed to be what I was looking for. I wanted something more specific than general advice, more actionable than uplifting sayings, more encompassing than personality tests, more reliable than trial and error, and more insightful than "do what you love for money." I was not after a magic formula but a solid framework to enable structured self-discovery and pilot me in my best direction.

After bouncing around like a pinball for nearly two decades, trying out new things and learning what I didn't like more than what I liked, I began thinking about simple questions to clarify what would make me feel fulfilled. These techniques worked for me and I want to share them with you.

This is not an autobiography. I've sprinkled in some details and example exercise results from my journey, but this book is for you to find your own path. My own reflective journey led me to write this book with the hope that it will have a net positive impact, affecting more lives for the better than not.

Appreciate the journey—your journey.

INTRODUCTION

We often pour our energy into our work, so much so that it can be mistakenly confused with identity. But what you do for work may not be your "life's work." What you do regularly may not regularly feel meaningful or fulfilling. What you do becomes a habit more than a conscious choice—one formed by spending so much time doing something without periodically pausing to ask: "Does this reflect who I am? Is this what I want?"

Does this sound familiar?

All too often, we become jaded, go through the motions, and lose sight of who we are and what we truly want in our professional *and* personal lives. It seems like human nature to dread the start of another workweek, another workday, and even another social engagement. With the amount of time we spend securely tucked in our routines, it's easy to miss the bigger picture. Consumed in day-to-day minutia, it's no surprise that we lose track of both the little things that bring us joy and the bigger things that we want to prioritize.

We don't always think of what *we* want in life and instead focus on what we know, what we've been told, and what we've learned to expect. We gravitate toward work that we excel at, but sometimes doing what we're good at or used to isn't what we're passionate about. As a result, it fails to bring fulfillment. We don't always pursue what we *want* and are left unsatisfied.

The good news is that we can always reground ourselves in who we are and revisit what fulfills us. Rather than thinking of our lives from a personal *or* professional standpoint, we can clear our minds to think of our lives holistically. We can pause to ask: "Is this what I want?" If it's not, we can change things.

You can *always* take a more active role in your life by consciously deciding where you want to spend your most precious resource—time. You can look at the bigger picture to identify what's most important to you and *strategically* make changes to feel more content and fulfilled.

Strategically is the operative word here, as strategy drives changes.

Strategy is all about considering the bigger picture to make thoughtful change. In a world of limited time and resources, a strategy is essential to identify the most important things to focus on.

As contributing researcher for Columbia Business School Willie Pietersen observes, "In a fantasy world of unlimited resources, we would not need a strategy. We could simply hurl resources endlessly at our problems and never be defeated. We would not need to take risks or make trade-offs and competition would be irrelevant."[1] In fact, this is why strategy exists in business.

Just as in business, we don't have unlimited resources in our lives (personal or professional). We have energy, time, and financial constraints—so why not apply the same strategic thinking to our personal lives?

We need to ask how we can position ourselves to make the most of our resources today and in the future. This requires us to:

- Understand who we are and what fulfills our existence—similar to a firm's values, purpose, and mission

- Recognize what we want—like a firm's vision and its corresponding objectives

- Identify how we'll get there—like a firm's goals

In this book, we will:

- Use identity and social research to help understand who you are and what fulfills you

- Apply a series of exercises to further explore individuality and what you want

- Develop an understanding of what you want to pinpoint what you specifically want to do

- Couple goalsetting with techniques for staying the course to get done what you set out to do

Inherent in this approach, we'll address two questions that are relevant not only to business strategy but also to your life strategy. They parallel the commonly asked business questions "Where will you play?" and "How will you win?" covered in A.G. Lafley and Roger Martin's *Playing to Win.*[2] These strategic questions will help you discover and pursue *your* passions in life, whether in your personal or professional life:

1) Where do I focus my resources?

2) How do I cultivate long-term contentment?

Think of your journey as a life strategy carried out to bring fulfillment. No strategic plan is linear. Just as business strategy involves iterations, musing, and debating, so too will your journey. There will be a series of reflective exercises to address question #1, helping you to identify and refine your focus in life.

A strategy is only as good as the paper it's written on if it's not well-executed. Implementing a strategy involves a plan, and plans are born to evolve. Just as business conditions alter and strategies pivot, personal conditions change and we adeptly adapt. That's why there will also be tools and guidance to address question #2, helping you to specify and pursue goals that deliver on your passion.

This book will encourage you to dive deeper within yourself and provide specific, actionable, and insightful advice to find and follow what makes you feel happy and fulfilled. It's organized into five sections:

1) Finding your passion

2) Understanding who you are

3) Clarifying what you want

4) Specifying what you want to do

5) Setting goals to do what you want

The book will include exercises to demonstrate the techniques and encourage real-time self-reflection. It's best to stop reading and complete the exercises as you go. The Passion Project companion workbook titled "My Passion Project: A Reflective Journal for Finding Fulfillment in Life" can be used to record responses to each exercise. Adjust the exercises to meet your needs. Be flexible and use whatever tools resonate most with you.

While the chapters need not be read in order, they are organized in roughly the order I found my direction. You may find that a different order is more useful in your life.

Regardless of which way you work through some or all of this book, there is no right answer. Do what helps you most.

PART I:

Passion

It is not in the stars to hold our destiny, but in ourselves.

— William Shakespeare

CHAPTER 1

Passion

What is passion? You might already have an idea of what passion means to you. It may conjure up strong emotions or little more than a shrug. Let's take a closer look at the word.

There are numerous definitions of *passion*. A simple search of Merriam-Webster reveals a spectrum of descriptors associated with passion: *love, anger, desire, even suffering.*[1] Passion comes from the Latin word *passio*, meaning suffering or enduring. In "The Metamorphosis of Passion", Rachel Weisbrot explains that its earliest meanings primarily referred to Christ's suffering, noting that Bach even wrote musical pieces called "Passions" inspired by the crucifixion. [2]

Subsequent meanings referred to enduring hardship in general. Around the 1300s, passion was a medical word referring to disease, which could have been anything from a minor ailment to a terminal illness or a psychotic episode. By the 1400s, passion represented intense emotions such as hatred or desire. Around the 1500s, the word took a sexual slant. These definitions continued to expand from the 1600s onward. [2]

Today, passion often reflects positive emotions such as like or desire. In recent years, there has been an increase in usage of the word in career contexts with advice to "follow your passion" or proclamations of "this is my passion."

However, in this book, we will distance ourselves from formal definitions and catchphrases that can be heavy with expectations or pressure. Instead, we will focus inward on the personal journey.

What is important is *not* a textbook or societal definition of passion, but that our pursuit of passion is our pursuit of what gives us a meaningful life—one we are proud of and glad we live. I hope that you find the journey to such fulfillment more inspiring and meaningful than any definition of the word in and of itself.

Finding Your Passion

Do you think you have a passion? Various tests and quizzes promise to reveal your passion within minutes, yet despite all the available tools making the process sound quick and easy, for many people, the path isn't that simple. Defining who you are and what you love and then pinpointing what to do with that information can be overwhelming and messy.

Regardless of whether you believe you have one or more passions or whether you believe you'll find it, it's worth distancing yourself from a word so laden with expectations. Instead, simply start thinking about what you want in your life to feel *fulfilled*. Fulfillment may be pursued in the form of relationships with others, hobbies, work, and/or any other areas of your life.

To begin to reframe passion and think solely about what you truly want in life, let's first distinguish contentment from happiness.

Why Contentment over Happiness?

What expectations do you have for your life? People commonly aim for happiness as an overall life goal or emotional state they expect to attain and remain in. But happiness is a momentary, fleeting feeling. Short-lived and temporary, happiness is not a permanent state that can be reached like some kind of nirvana. While happiness can often be influenced by personal choice, it does not sustain us. For example, you may feel happy if you decide to take a walk, go out for ice cream, or make vacation plans.

In contrast, contentment delivers a longer-lasting, deeper sense of being. The pursuit of passion can increase the frequency of happy moments in your life, but the true payoff is fulfillment. I think of fulfillment as long-term contentment created by living a life full of meaning.

As Courtney Ackerman, a contributor to positivepsychology.com notes, "Research shows that true happiness comes from pursuing more impactful and deeper things in life, like meaning. Simply trying to be happy does not really work in the long-term, although you might see short-term gains in happiness by just focusing your effort on being happier."[3]

Individual concerns with identity and expressing oneself have been found to contribute to meaning.[4] Experiencing a high degree of meaning can be achieved through valuing and pursuing what's most important to you—your passion(s). In this sense, the pursuit of passion can be reframed as simply the pursuit of meaning to achieve a sense of fulfillment. This removes the buzz and unhelpful associations, cutting to the core of what passion is and revealing that everyone can discover it.

Research on differences between a happy life and a meaningful life found that being a "giver" rather than a "taker" contributed to meaning.[4] It also found that happiness was not very closely related to meaningfulness. In fact, the researchers noted how increased levels of negative emotions, such as stress and anxiety, were associated with more meaningfulness but less happiness.

Why this apparent dichotomy? Meaningfulness can involve hardships and trade-offs, the payoff of which can bring deeper meaning to existence. Kaufman wrote about one study demonstrating that most meaningful events in life are either "extremely pleasant" or "extremely painful," and that both extremes stimulate contemplation.[5] Experiences, positive or negative, can be transformative when coupled with reflection.

You may have endured and overcome challenging times that brought tremendous meaning. Thinking back, these periods of your life may not have been very happy times but resulted in great achievement, pride, and fulfillment. You can use difficult past experiences and how you overcame them to shape who you want to be.

But remember that meaning and happiness are not mutually exclusive. Feelings of happiness can be unearthed at any time on your journey.

Self-Contentment

While we're on the subject of contentment, it's worth noting the importance of being content with yourself and what makes you *you*. *Amor fati* is a Latin phrase meaning "love of one's fate."[6] When you adopt an attitude of amor fati, you see everything in life as good or necessary. This includes pain and suffering as they are an inevitable part of the fabric of our lives.

It's the good and bad, ups and downs, joy and suffering, that build who we are. So, cherish the character of your fabric and those around you. This fabric is flexible and adaptive, a heavy coat protecting you from harsh elements or a light covering when you open yourself to vulnerability. It serves you in whatever ways you permit it. When you explore your identity, you open yourself up to greater contentment, but only if you allow yourself to be content.

Resist judging or resenting the texture of your fabric. Appreciating your unique history and personal experience helps you establish and accept your identity — the heart and soul of what makes you *you*. Pursuing what's meaningful to your heart and soul can lead to deeper contentment. When content with who you are, you give so much more to this world.

Fulfillment as a Need

Fulfillment is a basic need within us. We have an innate desire to grow as individuals to feel fulfilled. Maslow reflects this idea in his famous hierarchy of needs. In the textbook version, there are five tiers.

Bottom up, they are:

1) Physiological (biological basic needs like food, water, and sleep)

2) Safety (security in many forms such as social, emotional, and financial)

3) Love and belonging (relationships, acceptance, affection)

4) Self-esteem (regard for oneself)

5) Self-actualization (self-fulfillment)

The top need of the five-tier model, self-actualization, is a "growth" need because motivation *increases* as this need is met. *The more you feel you are reaching your potential, the better it feels and the more you strive to further your feelings of fulfillment.*

As an interesting aside, Maslow later posited that the order of the needs may be flexible depending on the individual; that is, the model is not a strict hierarchy. Your needs fluctuate over time. Job loss, divorce, and other external events impact where we are on the hierarchy. This can serve as a helpful reminder to be patient as you pursue a passion to strive for greater fulfillment. As is required with any strategy when working toward a goal, circumstances change and we need to adapt.[7]

So far, we've discussed the brief history of the word *passion* and the more recent buzz. We reframed passion as a pursuit of meaning to ultimately achieve a sense of fulfillment. We observed happiness as momentary while contentment is long term and derived from meaning. We also explored the philosophy that fulfillment is a basic need and innate in all of us.

Next, we'll look at how to pursue passion and how the concept of flow is connected to finding your passion.

CHAPTER 2

Pursuit of Passion

"Maybe I'll be a teacher in my second career," she said wistfully. She was an accountant.

I know an engineer who teaches, an analyst-turned-counselor, and others who went back to school to do what they enjoy—pursuing something radically different from their previous nine to five.

It's estimated that the average person changes their career five to seven times in their life.[1] While not all career changes are dramatic, an Indeed survey of U.S. workers found that 49% were. Of the remainder, 65% who hadn't made a dramatic career change were thinking about or had been thinking about switching in the past. Reasons for switching vary, but unhappiness in the job or sector was the top-cited reason in the survey.[2]

Whether your pursuit is spurred on by your current career trajectory or something else, there are certainly plenty of tools available to help. There are an estimated 2,500 different personality tests in the United States alone, not to mention a heap of career assessments, an assortment of passion-finding tools, numerous books on the subject, and a multitude of career-based blogs.[3] In fact, life coaching is a $1 billion industry in the U.S.[4]

Thanks to the myriad of assessments and tools, mentoring, feedback, and (last but not least) hands-on experience, we can learn more about ourselves and find our passion project. Yet, despite all of the resources available, we often follow the traditional, and unhelpful, path in our pursuit of our passion.

The Traditional Path

Through experience and external feedback, we uncover what we're good at and not so good at. This influences what we like and dislike. Other people often observe our skillsets and strengths, and we're socialized to pursue work in areas where we can apply them. As a result, we often:

- Do what we know or what we're good at

- Pursue what other people want for us

- Pursue what other people are doing

However, if we rely purely on the experience of others, we limit ourselves and we:

- Resist exploring new areas that may be ripe with opportunities

- Sacrifice our own fulfillment

- Compare ourselves to others despite being different people with different goals

On this traditional path, it can be easy to default to what we know and stagnate rather than grow. We can become accustomed to living according to the expectations of others, or even the expectations that we *think* others have for us. What's more, we compare ourselves to what others have, what they appear to have, or what we wish we had.

If we do stop to think about our passion, we often admire powerful role models who are brilliant, affluent, and work-obsessed—and who appear to love what they do day in, day out. Then, *we* strive to do what we love day in, day out too. This sounds noble but it's unrealistic and it's a trap, as you'll see next.

Day In, Day Out

For years, I expected to be fully engaged and absorbed in my daily work nearly all of the time. I previously considered a passion to be something you *always* wanted to work on and always wanted to think about when you weren't working. Then I realized this was closer to the definition of an obsession: "a persistent disturbing preoccupation with an often unreasonable idea or feeling".[5]

On the contrary, it's unrealistic to assume that we're destined to do an activity we enjoy all day, every day. So, reconsider whether it's realistic to feel great all day, every day. If you're a passionate hiker, you don't hike every waking hour. You plan routes, you train, you recover. If designing is your passion, you research, you sketch, you experiment, you procure, you fabricate. You perform a wide range of activities outside of the few you love most.

Not every moment is intended to be enjoyable in life, but the end result will be enjoyable if what you're doing is truly important to you. It can be helpful to lose the expectation of sustained happy moments and instead switch to the idea of living life in a way that's meaningful to you—a way that brings you long-term contentment by feeling fulfilled.

A Different Path

Let's contrast the traditional path to a different path—one where you actively pursue a passion. On this path, you seek to understand who you are, what you want, and what you want to do—to pursue a passion. Instead of looking purely to others for direction, you're in the driver's seat. You choose to let go of expectations and purposefully rethink what brings you fulfillment in life.

This path builds on what we know about happiness and meaning, and opts for the latter. Parts two to five walk this different path. But first, let's briefly explore what pursuing a passion can feel like.

Flow

Dr. Mihaly Csikszentmihalyi described what he calls *flow*, or the "optimal experience" in his popular book *Flow*. Subjects he studied "… described the feeling when things were going well as an almost automatic, effortless, yet highly focused state of consciousness".[6] I think of flow as a state in which time flies by, or you forget about time altogether, a state in which you are *absorbed*, not obsessed.

For me, flow is a state of intense focus or presence, full of delightful interest. It can happen during work or play — like when I'm solving an interesting problem, when I'm active outdoors, or when I'm socializing dogs. I liken flow to attaining the optimum balance between how engaged you are in something and how much you want to be doing that something. When you pursue a passion, you'll likely experience flow more often.

To some extent, you may experience fulfillment without experiencing flow. Facing difficult times, overcoming obstacles, and doing something because you feel morally compelled to can result in great pride and tremendous meaning and fulfillment. However, when you pursue a passion, meaning comes from something you're not only engaged in but also enjoy doing. It goes beyond compulsory obligation—it's something you actively elect to do with your time. This opens the doors to experience moments of flow and to experience further contentment in who you are.

A Construct of Flow

As you have seen, pursuing a passion may take different paths, one of which puts you in the driver's seat. We're reminded that passion brings enjoyment *over* time, not all the time, as feelings are transient and nothing is felt

Try It: **When Have You Experienced Flow?**

- Ask yourself: *When have I felt completely absorbed in what I was doing yet things felt effortless and highly enjoyable?* Jot down your top-of-mind responses.

day in, day out. Acknowledging this frees you to openly accept that your journey will have its demanding stretches and taxing obstacles. It allows you to appreciate the small happy moments and gratifying nature of flow along the way, and open yourself to contentment.

With passion reframed, we can move on to understand the root of where to find it: your identity.

PART II:

Who Are You?

To know thyself is the beginning of wisdom.

— Socrates

CHAPTER 3

What's Your Identity?

I hadn't stopped to think about my identity. I never gave much thought to all the different dimensions of my life. Instead, I erroneously associated who I was with my career—more specifically, my current position. When we spend most of our waking hours at work, it can be easy to think that our identity is synonymous with this one aspect of life. In this chapter, we introduce identity and its importance in finding fulfillment.

Identity and Its Importance

First, let's consider: *what is identity?* One of the most straightforward definitions for this relatively complex concept comes from Merriam-Webster: the set of qualities that make a person different from other people.[1] Identity is who you are—what makes you *you*. I liken identity to a sort of wrapper for your personality, values, and mission in life.

Knowing who you are lays the foundation for identifying what's meaningful to you. When you know who you are, you can much more easily determine what excites and fulfills you. When your actions align with your true self, you will find that a sense of peaceful contentment arises. This is the path to living your own life—the path to feeling fulfilled.

On the other hand, if we don't understand our own identity, it may cause us to not only chase things that don't align with who we are but also to neglect important dimensions in our lives. Instead of looking through a passive lens of "this is what I *chose* to do," understanding our identity through an active lens looks like: "this is what I *choose* to do with the time I have."

Who Are You?

What do you consider your identity to be? Whether you feel you've perfected it or fully achieved it is not important. What is important is that you are honest in how you think about yourself. It's also a question best not overthought. What is your top-of-mind response?

Caring for two terminally ill geriatric dogs, I considered my identity to be:

1) Loving wife

2) Caregiver of animals

No third dimension initially came to mind. No professional title excited me. Finally, I settled on:

3)   Adventurer, with a continual desire to see new places and experience new things

It struck me that none of these identities were occupation-related. My top-of-mind identities reflected a general lifestyle more than an obvious path to fulfilling a passion. And that's okay. Recognizing how you want to live is arguably the important part of how you want to identify yourself, which sharpens your focus on what will make you feel fulfilled. Acknowledging what fulfills you opens doors to new possibilities. Possibilities breed goals. Goals breed action. Action breeds results.

The following exercise will set the foundation for future exercises and help you understand what you inherently value and consider your mission. Try it out. Take your time and allow what comes up to come up. Be comfortable with the results and your identity that reveals itself.

Reminder: "My Passion Project: A Reflective Journal for Finding Fulfillment in Life" is the optional companion workbook that can be used to record your responses to exercises.

Try It: **What's Your Identity?**

- Ask yourself: *What's my identity?* Then jot down your top-of-mind responses in the form: *I consider my identity to be: ….*

- Think about why you answered the way you did. What is so important to you that it shines through?

- Reflect on your underlying values and motivations for your identity choice—how does your identity reflect your personality, personal values, or a previously unspoken mission? Then, note any significant themes that emerge.

At this point, these themes may be general and apply to a range of areas in your life. The themes that resonated from my earlier example were: a loving family, caring for others, and exploring new things. To specify what your identity themes mean, we'll delve into answering *"What do you want?"* in Part III.

But first, it's well worth taking the time to understand identity formation and its influences. If your current identity is not deliberate and committed to, answering what you need to feel fulfilled will be exceptionally difficult. Don't worry, we'll get there.

CHAPTER 4

Identity Formation

Identity is fluid, and forms over time. The things that you consider to be important parts of your identity change with age and experience. Understanding the basics of identity formation can help you gauge how prepared you are to identify and pursue a passion.

If you found it challenging to specify who you are in the *What's Your Identity?* exercise in the previous chapter, then knowing *where* you are in your identity formation journey and learning a little about the process may help you understand why.

Identity Statuses

How do you know where you are in your identity formation? Psychologist James Marcia proposed four identity statuses that explain the stages of the journey:

1) Diffusion

2) Foreclosure

3) Moratorium

4) Achievement[1]

Identity Statuses

Exploration

	Low	High
High (Commitment)	Forclosure: "I've made a choice without thinking."	Identity Acheivement: "I thought about it and I now know what I should do with my life."
Low (Commitment)	Identity Diffusion: "I don't know and I don't care what I'm supposed to do with my life."	Moratorium: "I'm thinking about what I should do."

James Marcia - Socio-emotional development

https://socioemotional.weebly.com/james-marcia.html[2]

Diffusion is when there is no commitment to an identity. In these cases, it may seem as if an individual is directionless.

Foreclosure reflects what some may call "settling." For example, in a career context, this may be a person who chose an occupation solely because a parent told them to pursue it.

Moratorium, on the other hand, is a state of active exploration where someone is still uncertain and undecided one way or the other.

Achievement signifies that an individual has not only explored but also decided what they want.[1]

Identity Formation Journey

We can learn something from others' identity-finding journeys. One longitudinal study of Finnish men and women analyzed identity statuses at ages 27, 36, 42, and 50. They assessed five dimensions — lifestyle, occupational career, intimate relationships, religious beliefs, political identity — and the study rolled the results into an overall identity status.[3]

- At age 27 (well past the age people typically embark on their first career), diffusion and moratorium were at the highest levels (~25% for each men and women).

- Fast forward to age 36—moratorium became uncommon as people started to commit to identity statuses through foreclosure or achievement. At age 36, foreclosure was the most common overall identity status (59% for men and 43% for women).

- At age 42, achievement became the most common overall identity status, but a significant number of men (37%) and women (29%) were in foreclosure.

- At age 50, roughly half of the participants had attained achievement as their overall identity status, yet a significant number of men (29%) and women (40%) were in foreclosure.

The typical progression toward achievement was diffusion to foreclosure to moratorium to achievement (D-F-M-A). In the *Handbook of Identity Theory and Research*, Schwartz et al. suggest that those who reach achievement are stable in their identities and that their life direction is not easily changed.[4] Your identity status may explain why some previous pursuits didn't quite stick.

 Try It: **Identity Status**

Answer these identity questions inspired by those in the Finnish study, to classify your identity status for these two aspects of your life: occupation and lifestyle.

Occupation

- Are you in the career you want for your life?

- How did you decide on your career?

- What quadrant of the *Identity Statuses* would you classify yourself for your occupation?

Lifestyle

- Are you living your life according to what's most important to you?

- What influenced you in deciding how you want to live your life?

- What quadrant of the *Identity Statuses* would you classify yourself for your lifestyle?

Before labeling where your identity falls as good or bad, remind yourself that identity formation is a journey. I found myself moving from diffused to foreclosed in my 20s. I moved from foreclosed to moratorium and back in my early 30s. While achievement is ideal, moratorium is a helpful second best, since it shows that active reflection is underway.

Multi-Dimensional You

Why might you not feel fulfilled if you solely develop the one dimension in your life that's most important to you? I hypothesize that it's due to the multitude of identity dimensions present in society (just look at the Finnish study) arising from our multitude of needs (look at Maslow's hierarchy). Your worldview is likely broader than, say, family, friends, or whatever your "top" priority is. You regularly see a wide range of possibilities and potential for broader impact — you see others doing things that intrigue and inspire you. We'll look further into these social influences next.

Social Comparison

There are two types of social comparisons: downward and upward. Downward comparisons occur when we compare ourselves to someone we perceive as "worse off" than us in some way. Upward comparisons do just the opposite—and they do not always make us feel worse. Comparing ourselves to individuals we admire can give us hope.[5]

Who do you look up to and why? Many of us may upwardly compare ourselves to family members or peers without good reason. Proximity is not a good reason for comparison. I ran into trouble when I compared myself to those I admired but whose pursuits didn't align with my own identity—my sisters, who were both studying to be engineers. I wholeheartedly knew I didn't want to be an engineer long before the morning of my graduation day, less than halfway through the first semester of my freshman year.

Krumboltz remarks on the profound consequences of deciding on something as important as occupation. Not only does it impact how we spend 8+ hours per day, 52 weeks per year, but it can affect where we live, our social circle, and even who we marry.[6] So, why are we pursuing identities we're not committed to?

External factors influence our journey. Krumboltz noted a lack of schooling on life planning and a lack of understanding of what adults do in their jobs. Another factor is the social pressure for prestige; for example, Krumboltz explains that people judge others on group membership (i.e., the occupation they are in (lawyer or doctor) versus how well they do the job).

While social comparison can sometimes be helpful, it can produce decoy passions that derail your pursuit of what's truly meaningful to you. Comparing yourself to an identity that doesn't fit your own will be of little use in self-fulfillment. When making upward comparisons, make helpful ones. Ask yourself if the individual is similar to who you want to be—if they are an inspiration to how you identify.

 Try It: **Admiration**

Reflect on who you truly admire. They can be people you know personally or those you have never met.

- Who do I admire?

- What do I admire about them? (What do they do? What character strengths do they exhibit?)

- How does what they do or who they are align with what I want to embody?

Next, consider how this inspires what you want for your own life.

1) Whose work resonates most with me (my identity)?

2) What makes their life's work so appealing to me?

3) What activities or work might carry that same appeal and excite me?

The next section expands on these exercises by pinpointing what you want in your life, having newfound awareness of:

- How you define who you are (*What's Your Identity?* exercise)

- How devoted you are to who you are (*Identity Status* exercise)

- How you look to others for inspiration (*Admiration* exercise)

Let's get to it.

PART III:

What Do You Want?

To be yourself in a world that is constantly trying to make you something else is the greatest accomplishment.

— Ralph Waldo Emerson

The identity exercises in the last chapter helped to reveal who you are. Now that you know how you identify and what's important to you, the next step is understanding what you want—your overall personal vision. This is the critical question behind the strategic question: *where do I focus my resources?*

The goal of Part III is to clarify key areas to concentrate on based on what's meaningful to you (i.e., your themes identified in Part II). Pursuing meaning leads to deeper contentment, and when you are content with who you are, you can be much more purposeful in going after what you want.

 Try It: **What Do I Want?**

Get to know yourself a little better without the pressures of terminology. Ignore passion, purpose, meaning, and the other terms that can create undue anxiety or unease. At this moment, let go of these things and focus on one simple question.

Take a deep breath and ask yourself: *what do I want?*

You'll notice what comes up organically and what emerges as prominent. Money might be a top-of-mind concern or nowhere on your list. Family time may consume more of your list than anticipated. Taking time to step back, let go of all expectations, and simply ask yourself what *you* want for your life is an act of self-compassion.

Don't be alarmed if you aren't certain at first, or if nothing comes up. Continue to relax and breathe deeply. Let the answers come naturally with time. Jot down your mind's answers, and accept them as they are—specific or vague, practical or idealistic.

Do you want to…

- Learn something new?
- Be physically fit?
- Live near a beach?
- Help people?

Articulating what you want, especially beyond general answers like those in the previous list, can be a challenge. This is where exploration helps, as uncovering and refining what you want requires reflection and contemplation.

Exploration is an individual journey. As you'll likely find out, it requires patience and self-acceptance. It can be time-consuming but also enlightening. Do not rush the process—clarifying your direction is an important step. Identity is an iterative journey, and it is not back-tracking but reassessing and growing.

The next two chapters serve as a guide to exploring what you want. They aim to kickstart your contemplation and offer an organic way of determining what you want to pursue. Be open to wherever these exercises take you. Bear in mind that a meaningful pursuit doesn't necessarily translate into financial wealth. While some people may think of ways to incorporate money into their life's work, don't *expect* it—if you do, you risk fogging the lens you are looking through to find meaning.

CHAPTER 5

Reflect

Reflection can uncover areas of interest that bring you the greatest meaning in life. Taking the time to consciously reveal those areas will help you pinpoint what you specifically want to do (Part IV). Here, we focus on defining meaningful interests.

Try any or all of these reflection approaches to better understand what makes you tick. These different approaches reveal interests and extract unspoken wants, so experiment with different ones to see what is revealed. Some may lead to *aha!* moments and a greater appreciation for who you are and what you're after. Observing where your mind drifts in a relaxed, free-flowing state can be insightful. Try these after meditation or as you unwind for the evening.

 Try It: **Reflect**

Note: This *Try It* section contains six different approaches to experiment with (in no particular order) and three wrap-up questions. To allow yourself sufficient time to reflect, consider doing one exercise per day for a week. Pause your reading and set reminders to try one approach each day. These tools are intended for careful guided reflection and not to be used all at once. Reflection can be an ongoing process. In the beginning, your answers may vary daily, especially if your identity is not quite fixed, so this process can be repeated in the future.

As you work through each approach, document your responses that resonate or spark something (with as little or as much detail as you find helpful) and skip those that don't.

Personality-Centered Approach

Certain tests reveal tendencies that can develop self-awareness and point to potential key interests.

- Try a free test, such as the Enneagram, which assigns you one of nine descriptive personality types (for example, Giver, Achiever, or Individualist).[1]

- Scan a free career inventory, such as the Career Personality Profiler on truity.com, to look for the types of activities or work you gravitate to.[2]

Maybe you're drawn to hands-on work or prefer solving existing problems versus exploring new frontiers. I was more interested in designing an advertisement than researching a new medicine because of the creative freedom and tangible results produced in short order. Be honest and think about why you like a specific area better than another without judgment.

Now consider how your tendencies make you gravitate toward certain interests. Complete these sentences:

- I value …

- I feel happy when …

- I am proud of my ability to …

How would you summarize what you gravitate toward?

Problem/Solutions-Centered Approach

You've likely heard a leader be asked "What keeps you up at night?" Use these questions to analyze what concerns you most in life:

- What questions or real-world problems keep me up at night?

- What organizations' missions resonate with me most?

- What gives my heart the biggest lift?

How would you summarize what you want to focus on?

Interest-Centered Approach

This approach centers on taking an inventory of what you like through prompts.

- What would I keep doing if I were a billionaire? These are likely interests you cherish already.

- What would I start doing if I were a billionaire? These are unacknowledged desires or interests you want to pursue. You can alternatively ask: If I was asked to start an organization, what would it do?

- What types of stories or experiences stay with me? Pull from news stories, anecdotes, accomplishments, or anything else that leaves an imprint and stays on your mind.

- What do I like to talk about? Reflect on recent conversations with family, friends, and anyone else in your life.

- What content do I engage with most? Think of the feeds you click, what you like to read, or what others tell you about because they know you'll be enthused by it.

How would you summarize what you're most interested in?

Remembrance Approach

This exercise borrows two questions from a Live Sonima meditation, and expands to uncover the unique gifts that bring you joy today.[3]

Through this approach you may realize that what you yearn for is what's been important to you all along.

Picture yourself at age five.

- Where do you shine?

- What do you love to do in your playtime? (What do you care deeply about?)

- What do you love about yourself at this age?

Repeat, picturing yourself at age 18, and again at your current age.

Now think about yourself today.

- What do you enjoy doing most in your free time now?

  Example:

  - Baking

  - Going for walks / hikes

- What are you yearning for now?

  Example:

  - To create more

  - To try new activities

- What interests (personal or professional) support what you yearn for?

  Example:

  - New product development

  - Art (pottery, drawing, or writing)

Life Experience Approach

Don't let what you already know about yourself go to waste. Interview yourself:

- How have my experiences influenced what's important to me?

- What do I want in my work? What's ingrained in me?

- What wouldn't I change about my work today?

- What puts me in a state of flow where I'm so absorbed that I forget about time or time flies by?

- Where do those closest to me (those I respect most and who know me best) see me thriving and most content?*

  *While your exploration is *your own*, the perspective of others who have your best interests at heart can serve as invaluable before significant jumping-off points, for example, to get an opinion on a potential career change or resource-consuming hobby.

Vision-Centered Approach

Do you find yourself wishing for something? Recurring thoughts are valuable reinforcing signals of what you truly want—whether it's a foster pet, a job, or learning that new thing.

Maybe your thought is a curious one: What if I … changed careers? Went back to school? Traveled the world? It could be an imaginary scene or a recurring daydream, picturing yourself somewhere or doing something; for example, envisioning yourself expertly interacting with people, or seeing yourself on a ranch. Or, it could be more like a drive, such as really wanting to work with kids.

The Vision-Centered approach evokes a visual representation of what you want. Something on paper may feel more tangible than those fleeting thoughts in your head.

Sketch or jot down your:

- Full-time dream work *(ignore pay)*

- Retirement dream *(what you see yourself doing without a paycheck)*

What are you enjoying? Who and what are you surrounding yourself with? (People? Animals? Machines? Computers? Microscopes? Art? Storefronts?) High-level visions are fine at this stage; narrowing down will come later, but take notice of any details that are tangible clues for what you specifically want to do (Part IV).

What did you learn about yourself from this approach?

Wrap-up

Review your findings.

1) What were your most illuminating questions?

2) What did you learn about what you want?

3) How does what you learned align with your themes from Part II (*What's your identity?* exercise)?

Among the most helpful questions for me were:

- What would I *keep* doing if I were a billionaire? *(Things I cherish and want in my life.)*

- What would I *start* doing if I were a billionaire? *(Things I want to pursue.)*

- What puts me in a state of flow, where I am so absorbed that I forget about time or time flies by? *(Activities that peak my engagement.)*

- Sketch or jot down your: Full-time dream work.

- Sketch or jot down your: Retirement dream.

The activities in this chapter relied on deliberate and structured introspection to unearth what most interests you and brings meaning to your life. The next chapter uses these findings to paint a more detailed picture.

CHAPTER 6

Imagine

One of the most powerful tools in exploration is your imagination. This chapter offers two main exercises. While both can be completed without trying any of the reflection approaches in chapter 5, prior reflection is useful to prime your thinking.

The first exercise, *Passion Finder*, aims to see you at your best. Just like you'd look for positive outliers or best practices in business strategy, here you'll highlight positive examples in your life to springboard off.

The second exercise, *World Stage*, operates under the premise that something worth sharing with the world carries greater potential for meaning for you. It extracts what conjures excitement within while prompting you to expand on what you want to share in life.

These are independent of one another and can be done in either order.

Exercises

Try It: **Passion Finder**

Take a deep breath. Let your mind wander to a time (personal or professional) when you felt extremely content with your life. Look for positive moments that relate to your areas of interest—those that you truly enjoyed and that brought you meaning or pride.

Now take a positive moment and savor it.

What were you doing?

_____

How do you remember feeling? *(Be specific, for example: calm, fulfilled, purposeful, successful, competent, etc.)*

_____

Who or what were you interacting with?

_____

Now put it all together. Why do you think you felt the way you did?

I felt _____ when I _____
_____ because I _____
_____.

Repeat these steps for other moments in your life.

Now think about all of the moments that came to mind. What do they have in common?

I am most content when _____

_____

_____.

What activities or roles might allow for more moments like these?

Example:

- Social work
- Program advisor (government or not-for-profit)
- Behavioral economics
- Facilitation
- Caretaking

What surprises you?

Example:

- Heavy social sector focus

 Try It: **World Stage Exercise**

Imagine the world is your audience.

- What are you excited to talk about? What do you most want to share?

Think TED talk topics…

Example:

- Landscape design—beautification principles
- Caregiving—how caregiving helps you and others
- Travel treasures—adventures you will never forget

Up to this point, the activities in this chapter painted a more vivid picture of what you want to focus on as your passion. The next step, which is short but important, confirms which interests most resonate with who you are and ensures that what you want is in accordance with who you are.

Taking a Pause

At this point, let's take a brief step back to refine your top interests and confirm they support who you are. Doing so can give you confidence that you're pursuing what interests you and solidify your true interests through purposeful, deliberate choice. It also ensures a strong foundation for the important *Ident-it-y Tree* exercise, which you'll do in the next chapter.

Try It: **Refine**

Use what you learned about yourself in **Reflect** (chapter 5) and **Imagine** (chapter 6) to narrow your findings down to two to five interests that represent what you want:

- What interests stand out, giving you the biggest "lift" thinking about? *(These will be the foundation for the Ident-it-y Tree.)*

- How do your interests align with your identity? With your values?

The next step is to identify how to apply these interests. We'll answer "What is *it* that you want to do?" in Part IV, the final part before setting goals and turning pursuits into action.

PART IV:

What Do You Want to Do?

Whatever you are, be a good one.

— Attributed to William Makepeace Thackeray

CHAPTER 7

Your *It*

How you spend your time is a reflection of who you choose to be. What is it that you want to do with your time? *It* refers to specific activities or actions you want to pursue, rather than job titles or roles. This is the critical question behind "How do I cultivate long-term contentment?" *It* ultimately translates your vision into an objective, and answers how you'll spend your most precious resource: time.

Choosing your *it* is more important than classifying the type of work or naming the role that suits you. You are comprised of more dimensions than just a work category, so there's no need to hastily shift what you want to do into a taxonomy. In this chapter, we'll transform interests into specific activities.

Ident-*it*-y Tree

The *Ident-it-y Tree* is an exercise that builds off the answers and interests identified in Part III (What Do You

Want?). We narrow in on specific activities aligned with who you are to bring you the most fulfillment. The tree lays out options for what you want to do. These option boxes are your decision points—where you decide which option best reflects how you spend your time. Each box, or decision point, is connected using branches.

This exercise can be done alone, but it uses previously covered techniques as a starting point.

 Try It: **Ident-*it*-y Tree**

Identify your *it*:

- Start your first branches by asking either "What interests me most?" or "Who (or what) do I want to help?" Using your results from the *Refine* exercise (chapter 6), customize the layers of your tree with options that reflect the interests uncovered in Part III (What Do You Want?).

- Next, start at the top of the tree and choose the option that reflects what you want to do at each level of the tree. Follow the branch of the option you select down to the next decision point until you reach the bottom.

  - ✐ *Tip:* Highlight the connecting branches (lines) and leaves (boxes) that you gravitate toward, including multiple paths if you're considering multiple options. There's no need to over-prune; just prioritize what is most important for you to explore.

Example: Using "Who do I want to help?" as the root question

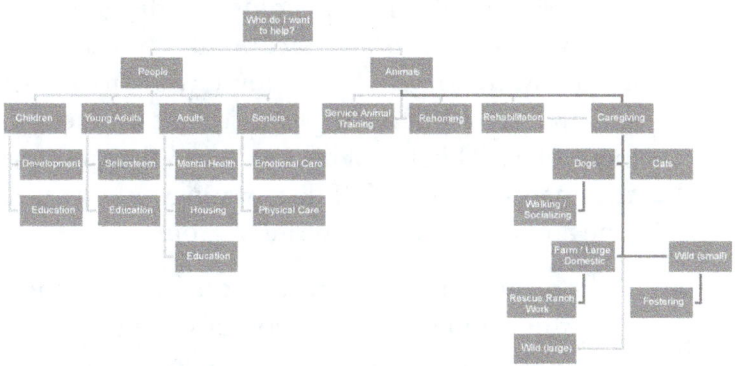

Here, the preferred direction is animal caregiving, with an affinity for dogs, farm animals, and small wild animals. Fulfilling opportunities might involve dog walking, volunteering at animal rescues, or in-home animal foster care.

Helpful reminders:

- Don't judge yourself for being you. You're applying your strengths and values to grow what's meaningful to you. Respect your cause—it's not for you to value one cause higher than another. There are over 7 billion people on this earth, each with unique gifts to offer. The world would be a very unhappy place if we all chose to do the same thing, so don't judge what brings you joy.

- Pursuit of meaning may mean not being paid well or even at all, depending on the industry or how willing you are to commit. For example, if you want to write but don't want to invest resources into publishing and serious marketing, then you will likely not become a full-time author. You may feel more fulfilled writing in your free time and joining a local writers' group.

- There's no rule that you need to abandon everything and pursue a major life change. In fact, sometimes, the right path is discovering more happy moments in your current day-to-day life while making room to cultivate greater meaning outside your present obligations. Consider this perspective as you find your *it*.

L-it-mus Testing

What emotions do you experience when you think about the *it* you selected? What's stopping you from going after what you've identified? Testing your passion before you pursue it can give you a better idea of whether *it* will contribute to you feeling fulfilled.

 Try It: **Visual Litmus**

- Visualize doing the passion you selected *today*, in this very moment, and fill in the blanks:

  I see myself _____ and I feel _____.

  Tip: Try asking this at various times during the day, especially when you feel tired or tense— you may surprise yourself by being excited to do something despite your mood.

- Visualize how you'd feel doing what you selected six months or a year from now and fill in the blanks:

  This has impacted my quality of life by _____, and I am feeling _____.

Revisit your cause if you feel apathetic, stressed, or drained. If you feel anxious, try to understand why and soothe your anxiety by looking at the big picture: you're taking small steps to pursue what's important to you. Concerns about time constraints, obligations, and competing priorities are expected. (Part V discusses honoring your needs and lays out the process to bridge any gaps, which will help you manage any concerns.)

Perhaps the best way to know how you'll feel is to try it. Look for an efficient and low-risk means to easily act on what you want. It can be as formal as job shadowing or a volunteer engagement—or as informal as learning from online videos. As you try something, consider:

- How do you feel about what you tried?

- How quickly did the time go by?

- How has your perspective changed?

In this chapter, we discussed how to identify what *it* is that you want to do and encouraged litmus testing. Next, we'll cover some of the surprising reactions you may have during the litmus testing.

CHAPTER 8

Revisiting What You Want to Do

Sometimes, after trying (or even visualizing) something, you realize it's not what you expected—just like a poor job fit, although the reasons we'll focus on here are personal rather than professional or interpersonal. What you thought you wanted to do may not excite or fulfill you in the way you imagined.

This can happen if you're striving to meet expectations set by you or others that don't fit who you are. It can also happen if there is an unreconciled difference between what you say you want and any deeper held beliefs or desires. You may also question whether what you want to do constitutes a job or a side hobby at this point in your life. We'll discuss all these scenarios in this chapter.

Before you read on, write down your response to "What is *it* that you want to do?" from the previous chapter. This will serve as a reference as you read on.

Doing, Not Proving

Excitement should come naturally. Your *it* should be so natural that it feels as though you're conveying who you are. Your *it* is not about selling who you think you should be or who others expect you to be. Living according to your true identity means there's no need to put up a facade. It means looking forward for the sake of *doing, not proving,* what you set out to do. If you feel you have to prove something and aren't eager to do it, then revisit the earlier sections (*Who Are You?* and *What Do You Want?*).

Disconnects

At times, there can be disconnects between what we want to do to feel happy and fulfilled—and what we desire for our lives. Asking what you desire for your life is another way of asking what you want to do in life, but it can reveal a gap between what you say will make you happy and what you *feel* you *need* to do.

The word "desire" evokes a dreamier perspective than "want", and it can help elicit unresolved feelings from deep down. The word "desire" can uncover a more general or long-term vision you're looking to fulfill, or think you *should* fulfill (the latter being an ideal you'll want to reconcile).

Try It: **Finding Disconnects**

- Ask: *What do I desire for my life?*

- Is there a difference between what you say you desire and what you identified in the earlier *Ident-it-y* exercise? If there is, consider why.

Here are some thought patterns that shed light on these disconnects:

"It's so far away."

If what you desire seems unreachable, ask yourself why. It may be intimidating because it seems so far from where you are today. This is where goal setting will help. Just because something takes time doesn't mean it needs to be discarded. Taking a few small steps may be enough to bring you joy, or may embolden you to take more small steps and so on. Progress takes time.

"It's not realistic."

If this is your concern, it's important to understand what *specifically* doesn't seem realistic.

For example, the way I envisioned animal rescue work seemed very unrealistic for my own life. I forced benchmarks where they shouldn't exist because "my desire" reflected what I thought I *should* do. Specifically, I inadvertently compared what I wanted to do (small-scale intensive care) with what others were doing (large-scale general care). It was an unreasonable comparison because it wasn't what I wanted to do. I had to reconcile what I held as a false ideal (what I thought I should desire) with what I truly wanted.

For another person, something may seem realistic because of current commitments or time constraints. Goal setting will again help here, guiding how you prioritize and spend precious time and energy.

Doing things in the way that fits your life is unique to *you*. Stick with what you value and the approaches that work for you. Understand and *respect* this, so you can be happy and fulfilled with a sustainable impact. Acknowledging values and finding balance is covered more in **Goal-Setting Guidelines** (chapter 10).

"It's so unlikely."

Another reason for something seeming unrealistic may be due to its likelihood, for example, the probability of achieving great fame. In this case, understand why doing what you love isn't enough. Seeking fulfillment is about contentment in *being and feeling* enough, rather than competing to *have* enough.

Alternatively, something may seem unlikely due to a lack of confidence. Question the root of why you feel something is unlikely. Understand if insecurity is blocking you from pursuing something truly important to you.

As we've seen, understanding our deeper desires and reasons for them can reveal unacknowledged feelings and beliefs that need challenged. Investigate these desires with curiosity. Try to work out any differences between what you *want* to do to live a happy, fulfilled life and deeply held notions. Your findings may alert you to how true (or not) you're being to yourself and indicate the need for more reflection.

Delineating Job and Hobby

Sometimes, you need to do further exploration to understand whether your goal should be something you do as a job or as a hobby. The only "right" answer here is what is right for you. A passion is not something to be done day in and day out, but in balance.

Here are three questions to assess how you might want to pursue your interests:

1) Do you want to do this full-time, every workday?

2) Will you put in the effort to get paid to do this?

3) Are you willing to accept the amount you will likely be paid?

These questions can be helpful at any time on your journey. They can also apply to the initial reflection exercises through the *Ident-it-y Tree*. Ideally, you should be clear on whether you want to do something as a job or as a hobby before setting goals (Part V).

When I answered these questions using my results from the *World Stage* exercise, I stopped after the first question because my answer was obvious. I did not see full-time (or even part-time) travel as something I wanted to do every day. So for me, travel was a hobby and treated as such in my goal setting.

 Try It: **Revisit**

- Write down what *it* is that you've decided you want to do.

- What's changed from what you wrote down at the beginning of this chapter?

Having identified and examined what you want to do, the next step is to start planning the actions you'll take to make your *it* a reality. The next part of this book focuses on goals and how we get to where we want to be.

PART V:

Doing Is Seeing Is Believing

The future depends on what you do today.

— Mahatma Gandhi

CHAPTER 9

Goal-Setting Foundations

Goal setting is the tool for bridging what you want to be doing in the future with your reality today. It defines *how* you'll reach your destination so you *can* reach your destination.

You now have a well-tuned vehicle: you are in tune with your identity. Based on your interests and what you want, you've chosen a destination: your *it*—what you want to do. Now you need to map your route: how will you get there?

This is where goals come in. They serve as mileposts on your route, indicating where you are and how far along you are on your journey. So, how do you map the route that's best for you? You plan your route based on your gaps and needs to set yourself up for success.

Think about the very definition of business strategy. Authors George Bradt et al. of *The New Leader's 100-Day Action Plan* describe it this way: "At its core, strategy is simply generating and selecting options that will close the gaps between the objectives and current reality... Strategy boils down to selecting which options to pursue and which options not to pursue."[1] Similarly, consider what gaps must be addressed for you to reach your destination. As you formulate your goals, you'll incorporate the best options to successfully close these gaps while keeping your personal needs in mind.

Identifying Gaps and Needs

Only the present matters when making a change. You can use the present to map out something in the future, but a solid plan depends on rooting yourself in the reality of here and now. This means acknowledging your current state and identifying any gaps and needs that should be addressed. Comparing what you have today with what you want will uncover these gaps.

Recall the *Identity Status* exercise in chapter 4 that asked:

- For occupation: Are you in the career you want for your life?

- For lifestyle: Are you living your life according to what's most important to you?

If you answered no to either question, you have a gap. Gaps reflect what you want that you don't have today. They can be external, like a culture incongruent with your values or lack of support for your personal development, or internal, such as an unmet need to express autonomy and try new things.

Just as importantly, you should examine what's going well. These are the things you likely need to succeed or may not be willing to give up in your pursuit of fulfillment—things like financial stability or work-life balance. These are already-met needs you'll want to protect. Understanding them allows you to derive gratitude from what you have and not lose what you value today. It grounds you in suitable goals and helps you manage risk, preventing you from walking away from something prematurely.

For example, in a situation of healthy work-life balance, one of your goals may center around doing more of what you want outside of work before pursuing a major career change that jeopardizes your existing work-life balance. If you have less free time outside of work and value job security or financial stability, one of your goals may be to sharpen your transferable skills at work to do more of what you want to do in your job. In the latter scenario, the goal works within your existing constraints to lay the groundwork for a desired future state.

Identifying your gaps and needs is fundamental to setting goals. You should weave your findings into the goals you develop to minimize the risk of unmet needs and blockages. The next exercise helps you pinpoint key gaps and needs to address.

 Try It: **Identifying Gaps and Needs**

Thinking of your *it*, consider:

- What's going well today that you don't want to give up (met needs)? How might you incorporate this into your goals?

- What's missing—what don't you have today (gaps)? How might you incorporate this into your goals?

Now you've identified these needs and gaps, the next step is to make sure your gaps are closed while honoring your needs.

Closing Gaps while Honoring Needs

Closing gaps doesn't necessarily mean making big changes. Small, simple changes can impact your physical, emotional, social, and intellectual wellbeing. Examples include spending more time with loved ones, taking a daily walk, doing a 5-minute daily gratitude exercise, setting electronics aside when someone is talking, and signing up to volunteer.

What steps can you take *now*? *The Matrix* tool helps you map out practical changes to do more of what you want to do in your life. Thinking about specific activities, categorize what you want to do more of and what you can do less of. You can identify actions that increase fulfilling moments and decrease resources spent on less fulfilling moments. We'll use this to construct goals in chapter 11.

 Try It: **The Matrix**

- Using the results from the *Identifying Gaps and Needs* exercise, complete the matrix.

  Guidance:

  - Things going well today that you don't want to give up (met needs) are things you want to *keep up* (upper-left quadrant).

  - Things missing in your life today (gaps) are things you want to *start doing* (lower-left quadrant).

  - The right quadrants represent things in your life today that risk interfering with you acting on what you want to do.

	I like ...	**I don't like ...**
I do ...	**Professional** *What should I keep doing in my professional life?* **Personal** *What should I keep doing in my personal life?* *Keep it up*	**Professional** *What should I stop doing in my professional life?* **Personal** *What should I stop doing in my personal life?* *Stop*
I don't do ...	**Professional** *What should I start doing in my professional life?* **Personal** *What should I start doing in my personal life?* *Get started*	**Professional** *What should I still refrain from doing in my professional life?* **Personal** *What should I still refrain from doing in my personal life?* *Keep it that way*

Adapted from webinar resource [2]

Example:

	I like …	**I don't like …**
I do …	**Professional** Program management **Personal** Regular exercise *Keep it up*	**Professional** Tactical implementations **Personal** Extensive weekend cleaning *Stop*
I don't do …	**Professional** Strategic planning facilitation **Personal** Reading up on behavioral sciences Volunteering *Get started*	**Professional** Technical troubleshooting **Personal** Grocery shopping during peak busy times *Keep it that way*

The results from *The Matrix* exercise can be directly incorporated into the goals you set (chapter 11):

- **Keep it up:** These are things going well that you don't want to give up (needs to honor), so build time for these in your goals.

- **Get started:** These are things critical to being able to do what you want to do (gaps to close). Ensure you set goals to implement these.

- **Stop:** These are things that risk interfering with your goals. As much as practical, make sure these things are *not* done, so they don't take time away from what it is you want to do.

- **Keep it that way:** These are things to be aware of—don't let them creep back into your life and take time away from what it is that you want to do.

We now know the foundational elements to include in goals so we can safeguard needs while still addressing gaps. Before we draft our goals, let's review some guidelines. When properly structured, goals motivate us and keep us on track.

CHAPTER 10

Goal-Setting Guidelines

Goals get a bad rap, but they are not the enemy. When well-written, they inspire and serve as guideposts on the path to fulfillment. Goals are the mechanism to operationalize strategy in business and in life; they help us turn what sounds good on paper into action and tangible results. In this chapter, we'll explore guidelines to set meaningful goals, which we can then use to draft goals (chapter 11).

Goal-Setting Guidelines

The Matrix in the last chapter helped us think through what actions we might take to do what we want to do in life. Here, we cover guidelines to write goals that are clear and motivating.

Set Your Own Goals

It's up to you to determine your own life goals, which will invariably be different from everyone else's because your identity is unique. Recognize that your goals are different from the goals you think others have for you. Ensure you set goals that will make *you* happy, not those you think *should* make you happy or those you think will make others happy.

Set Goals, Not Expectations

Set goals, *not* expectations. Goals are the steps you need to get where you want to be (your chosen destination). Expectations are assumptions. They often assume (with little merit) that we should already be where we *want* to be. If this is the case, we're bound to fall short. Of course we'll fall short when we've done nothing to try to achieve where we want to be. It is hard work through goals, not expectations, that takes us to our destination.

Start Small

It can be tempting to continually think of your vision as your end goal. Here, you see the forest but don't appreciate the individual trees that comprise it. It's executable, tangible goals that turn vision into reality.

When setting goals, use a "small steps" mindset. A long-term vision becomes manageable when you treat each day as an opportunity to get one step closer to living your vision. Even 20 minutes a day can add up quickly. Think of what you can accomplish in 20 minutes—pick out a healthy recipe and make the grocery list for dinner, look up a school's course offerings, update a section of your resume, or walk around the block. Small tangible goals are key to staying on track and motivated.

Stay SMART

SMART stands for Specific, Measurable, Achievable, Relevant, Time-bound. This acronym is common in business settings, so why wouldn't we hold the same standards in our personal lives?

- **Specific:** This makes it clear what success looks like. If you want to obtain a certification, state what area you will be certified in and where you will do the certification.

- **Measurable:** It's evident whether you accomplish it. A degree or certificate, data from a running watch, and recorded volunteer hours are all measurable.

- **Achievable:** It's generally more encouraging to set a goal you perceive as within reach. For example, rather than just setting a revenue target 5 years away, set goals for 6 and 12 months' time.

- **Relevant:** This relates to your strategy—in our case, seeking fulfillment.

  Relevant refers to setting a goal that aligns with what *it* is you want to do.

- **Time-bound:** This accounts for how long it will realistically take to do something. Don't give yourself an exorbitant amount of time (years) if something should take months, and vice versa.

It can be tempting to pursue things tangentially relevant to what you want. For example, I was interested in learning more about not-for-profit program management. As an avid learner, I almost jumped into working toward a certification but realized it was not required for what I wanted to do. It was a nice-to-have, but it would have constrained my time and delayed me from doing something sooner using the skills I already had. I would have been pursuing the certification for its title rather than its value. Try to prioritize your focus on what gives you the greatest fulfillment.

Try It First

Consider setting a goal to try something out, even if there is no commitment attached. Generally, there is no major action taken in business without some sort of prototype, pilot, user feedback, test, or experiment. Trying things helps us distinguish where to commit resources without significant upfront emotional or financial investment.

Use a trial perspective, taking steps big enough to get your feet wet but small enough to limit the psychological pressure to proceed. There is no pressure except what you put upon yourself. You're not a quitter if you elect to stop because this is an experiment—one discrete step of a larger comprehensive process. It's not the end of the process nor the destination. It's a stopover.

Embed trying or learning something new into the goals you set. You'll discover more about what you like and dislike, and better align how you spend your time with how you want to spend your time.

Know Your Tendencies

Structure your goals to motivate you. Knowing what motivates you is a powerful piece of information that will set you up for success. Gretchen Rubin's Four Tendencies framework categorizes individuals into one of four behavioral leanings, and each is connected to what drives us:

- Upholders (tell me what should be done)
- Questioners (give me justification)
- Obligers (hold me accountable)
- Rebels (let me do it my way)[1]

Goeke summarizes the tendencies as follows: Upholders are self-disciplined and like rules; Questioners like purpose and should be reminded of the significance of their pursuit; Obligers meet others' expectations and are best held accountable by external influences, such as a friend or boss; and Rebels value freedom and like to respond to challenges but without pressure.[2]

Keep your tendency in mind as you set your goals. I am a Rebel—I like autonomy when solving problems, which I work into how I word my goals. For example, rather than commit to swimming every Friday and Sunday afternoon, I set a goal to swim twice per week. While I eventually found and followed a somewhat regular schedule, I am motivated knowing that I have the freedom to do things at different times on different days. This gives me the flexibility I need to be successful.

Depending on your tendency, you may benefit from a checklist or vision board, or asking a friend to check up on your progress on a particular date or time interval. Establish your goals in a way that sets you up for success.

Change Your Attitude or Change Your Direction

Before setting goals to significantly change your life, consider your options—goals can support you in changing your attitude or changing your direction.

How does what you want to do align with what you're doing already? If similar, you can do the following to reframe your present position:

- Increase happiness and cultivate joy from the little

things, viewing everyday tasks and interactions as opportunities to generate more meaning in your life.

- Acknowledge what you don't like in your current situation but balance it by acknowledging what you *do* like.

- Look for similarities between what you like today and what you want to do tomorrow to cultivate meaning.

- View your work as a stepping stone for what you're interested in the long term. For example, with an affinity for metrics development, I saw the potential to apply my experience to not-for-profit pro bono work.

If there are too few similarities between what you do today and what you want to do, too little opportunity to develop transferable skills, or too many conflicts between your current situation and your values, your goals may need to reflect a more drastic change in direction.

Respect Your Values and Find Your Balance

On a recent airline flight, the steward announced, "Customer service is our passion. Safety is our priority." When setting goals, look to your values to know your top priorities and design your goals around them. Passion should not come at the cost of your happiness and that of those you love. This is where priorities are your guide.

You'll find a balance that works by considering how your goals not only impact you but those closest to you. At one time, I needed multiple people to point out that if I worked with a particular not-for-profit, I would carry a heavy emotional burden. Despite being a worthy cause, an element in their environment conflicted with one of my convictions. There was no doubt that I would bring residual stress home to my personal life.

Remember to consider how emotions, fatigue, and stress may inadvertently spill over into your relationships, so you can maintain the balance you need. If you work full time, your balance might be two hours every weekend spent pursuing what you love. Two hours to cultivate joy is better than zero, and that number can change as your life and other priorities permit.

Note: Balancing your time between various areas you care about doesn't put you at a disadvantage in self-fulfillment. Remember identities are multidimensional, so it's sensible to give a part of yourself to multiple dimensions. How you choose to allocate the sum of your energy is a personal decision.

With clarity on how to write meaningful goals that both motivate us and keep us balanced, we start drafting goals next.

CHAPTER 11

Drafting Goals

Now you have the tools and it's time to draft goals to help you on your path to greater fulfillment. Goals are the working layer underlying the strategic question *How do I cultivate long-term contentment?* They are the means to implement your strategy, stipulating what resources you will use, how, and at what times.

Roughing Out Goals

You can use this next exercise for multiple branches on your *Ident-it-y Tree* (chapter 7). The purpose is to identify steps (goals) to bridge what you do now with what you want to do in the future.

 Try It: **Roughing Out Goals**

Using your *Ident-it-y Tree* results, concisely state what you want to do to feel more fulfilled—what passion you will pursue:

- *I want to …*

Example:

- I want to help rescued dogs by providing love, exercise, and enrichment.

Next, state how you'll start doing this using "I will" statements. These are clear, immediate actions you can take, especially things to try if you have multiple projects that interest you.

To get started, refer to your results from *The Matrix* exercise in chapter 9 to recall the things you want to keep doing, start doing, and stop doing. Think about how doing these things can enable your accomplishing what you want to do.

Consider how to gain the knowledge and skills required to pursue what you want to do, such as:

- Researching subjects (credentials of those you admire who are already doing something similar to what you want to do, career paths, fields of study, schools or programs, etc.)

- Exploring subjects (lessons, shadowing, informational interviewing, volunteering, etc.)

- Acquiring skills (formal or informal schooling, training, etc.)

- Investigating opportunities (job openings, grants, community support services, etc.)

Now craft some statements using this form:

- *I will ... so I can ....*

Example:

- I will research not-for-profits so I can find the mission and location that fits me best.

- I will write an article on career advice to see if I might enjoy coaching.

Finally, state what you need in order to identify the reinforcing support or motivators that will facilitate you taking action. Think about how you like to work and get things done (independently, by declaring commitments, etc.), and the social and physical environments you thrive in (communal, open, quiet, outdoor, etc.). Don't force yourself to acclimate to a surrounding if you can do the equivalent work in a setting more conducive to your success.

Now compose some statements using the following form:

- *I need ... to ...*

Example:

- I need to volunteer in an environment that values cleanliness and animal socialization.

- I need a deadline so I don't let things drag on and diminish my happiness.

- I need funds to self-publish.

- I need to find a mentor with experience in strategy.

Your *I want to …*, *I will …*, and *I need …* statements lay the foundation for your goals. They clarify what you will do and what you need along the way. Before putting pen to paper, let's try visualizing your success.

A key activity in business strategy is scenario planning, during which businesses approximate what the future might hold using assumptions and simulations. Hre, your simulation will be envisioning your ambitions coming to fruition.

 Try It: **Success Visualization**, adapted from *Goal Visualization*, created by Hugo Alberts (Ph.D.) and Lucinda Poole (PsyD)[1]

1) Think about what you want to do to feel more fulfilled. Refer back to your *"I want to …*, *I will …*, and *I need …* statements from the *Roughing Out Goals* exercise.

2) Picture yourself one month from now. What does success look like? What actions have you taken to get this far?

3) Picture yourself six months from now. What does success look like? What actions have you taken to get this far?

4) Imagine you've reached your goal. What does success look like? What does it feel like? What actions have you taken to get this far?

5) What additional actions or goals did this exercise help you identify?

Drafting Goals

With rough goals and an idea of how you envision moving forward, it's time to put pen to paper. The process of setting goals is nonlinear and iterative as you try things, explore further, and create new goals based on what you accomplished and learned along the way. The future never turns out the way we expect, but goals ground us in what's important to us. With goals, we are less likely to lose our way, and more likely to achieve what we set out to do because we have focus and a plan.

 Try It: **Drafting Goals**

The *Roughing Out Goals* and *Success Visualization* exercises likely gave you a solid start on what you need to do next. Now it's time to pull everything together.

- Think of one or two things you can do now to start pursuing your passion.

- Draft two or more goals using the SMART format (Chapter 10), which will start you on what *it* is that you want to do to live a more fulfilled life.

Example:

- Self-publish self-help book by September 30. Complete initial draft by June 30 and developmental edit by July 31.

- Volunteer a minimum of 4 hours per month at a no-kill animal shelter, starting March 13 through year-end.

Things rarely turn out exactly as planned, but with the right goals drafted, you can always pursue what you want to do. The journey and the small steps we take can be as fulfilling as a destination, especially when we learn from and seize all the twists and turns along the way. As the African proverb goes, "Smooth seas do not make skillful sailors."

The final chapter discusses how we can keep motivated through the twists and turns.

CHAPTER 12

Keeping Motivated

In business and life in general, actions speak louder than words. If you want to pursue something that you truly value, then put your words and goals into action. It's a virtuous cycle: *doing* will result in you *seeing* change, which will result in you *believing* in what you can do.

You can start now, as only the present matters when making a change. In the words of Mahatma Gandhi, "The future depends on what you do today." Let's explore a few things that it takes today to stay the course for tomorrow.

What It Takes to Stay Motivated

It Takes Reminding

Remind yourself what you're doing and why. Develop a mission statement, mantra, or tagline to keep the importance of what you're doing alive and in perspective.

It doesn't need to be shared and is purely for your motivation. Alternatively, try to reground yourself in what's most important, especially as you pursue new goals.

 Try It: **Grounding**

Use a bucket list to refocus on what's most important in your life, and to more deeply appreciate what's right in front of you.

Goal Setting	Reflection	Impact
What would I want to accomplish if I had only one year left to live?	*Why is this important to me? How will it make my life more meaningful or grow my contentment?*	*How important is this goal to growing my contentment?*
1.		
2.		
...		

Adapted from the 'Before You Die' Bucketlist Worksheet[1]

It Takes Confidence

To achieve goals, growth is vital. So, believe that you can develop your talents, which is known as a "growth mindset", rather than thinking they are innate, a "fixed mindset". Reset your frame of mind, reminding yourself that every day is an opportunity to learn and grow.

Author and Professor of Psychology Carol Dweck sums up the research on growth vs. fixed mindsets:

> Individuals who believe their talents can be developed (through hard work, good strategies, and input from others) have a growth mindset. They tend to achieve more than those with a more fixed mindset (those who believe their talents are innate gifts). This is because they worry less about looking smart and they put more energy into learning.[2]

Assure yourself that you can grow and lean on your support network for help. Think of it as a self-fulfilling prophecy.

It Takes Effort

Regardless of what you choose to call it—finding your passion, seeking self-fulfillment, achieving self-actualization—it takes work, drive, and personal commitment. Even when you have goals to keep you on track, one of the biggest challenges is staying motivated to act on them.

Imagine training for a triathlon. You may prefer biking over swimming over running, so certain training days may take more effort than others. But the end game is what keeps you training, and keeps your training well-balanced. Though some elements may be more fun than others, each is important and necessary to cross the finish line. And that's what excites you—the thought of crossing the finish line, knowing you've accomplished what you set out to do.

Diligently remind yourself that results take effort and effort takes time. Accepting this will make things go more smoothly, and you'll learn to be your own best friend.

 Try It: **Finish Line Visualization**

Remind yourself of where you want to be. Close your eyes and vividly imagine how a near-term success would feel. Harness these emotions to re-engage and reignite excitement. Repeat for a longer-term success.

It Takes Courage

Staying on track means springing into action to do things even when you don't feel like it. In this case, a support network can cheerlead and drive you to action when you're lacking confidence or feeling less inclined. Your gut is also a great source of motivation, encouraging you to do something related to your goals when you're feeling anxious. Gut instincts often come as an urge, thought, or "I should" statement. They may nudge you to take a walk, call a loved one, sign up for a cause, or apply for that job.

Mel Robbins uses The 5 Second Rule: "5-4-3-2-1-GO!" to gather the courage and motivation to act. Counting helps to redirect your focus while physical movement helps you take decisive action, so at the end of your count your thinking is clearer and you are inspired to act.[3]

Try It: **The 5-Second Rule**

When you have a gut instinct to do something in support of your goal, count backward from 5 seconds, physically move, then act on that instinct.

It Takes Honesty

Staying the course also requires honesty. How do you know if you're being honest with yourself? Check in to reassess your goals and affirm that you're spending your resources (time, energy, and/or money) where you want to. Are you still enjoying yourself? What are you feeling? How is what you're doing impacting those around you?

Although working on something may not always excite you, be sure that the goal itself is still meaningful to you. You may determine that a goal no longer aligns with what you want or need to focus on in life due to current circumstances and priorities, and that's OK.

Check-ins are critical when expending precious resources to pursue your interests. There's something to be said about maintaining self-awareness and taking stock of whether the way you're spending your time still makes you happy. It's neither healthy nor realistic to expect consistent excitement, but you should still feel something from small victories, knowing they're for the right reason—taking you one small step closer to your vision.

 Try It: **Check-In**

Choose one of your goals to work on for a few minutes. After at least 5 minutes absorbed in the task, ask yourself:

- Am I enjoying this?

- Is this how I want to be spending my time right now?

- What emotions am I feeling?

- What bodily sensations am I feeling?

The last question provides an important clue about what that task means for your health and happiness. As neuroendocrinology researcher and Professor Robert Sapolsky points out in his popular course *Introduction to Human Behavioral Biology*, "Sometimes what's going on in your head will affect every single outpost in your body."[4] If you tell yourself you feel happy but your body is tense and telling you otherwise, you may need to get closer to your true emotions. If you feel content and your body is relaxed and fluid, that's a more consistent story.

It Takes Self-Care

Last but certainly not least, staying the course takes self-care. We must do our best with the tools we have. This includes taking care of those tools. You will do greater good when you care for yourself and your own needs.

I initially ignored the general importance of self-care and achieved worse results. When I think back to caring for our geriatric lab, Bayla, I was at my best when I was both physically and emotionally refreshed. Realize that taking time to reset is how you become more productive—no one can sustain doing one thing all day, every day.

Self-care is personal and should cater to you. This may mean anything from daily meditation to scaling a hobby or business differently compared to anyone else. It may mean giving yourself more freedom or less pressure. For example, if you're aware that you tend to be more hydrated and energized in the afternoon, you don't need to force yourself to exercise in the morning. You don't need to wait to write in the evening if you feel like writing now. Be considerate of your needs and what will make you the happiest and most productive in the process. Pursue fulfillment in the way that works best for you.

With established meaningful goals and guidelines for staying motivated throughout your journey, you are well-positioned to pursue what fulfills you. Before we finish our journey together, let's take a moment to recap everything you've done to set yourself up for success.

CONCLUSION

From Pains to Gains

Defining who you are and what you love, then deciding what to do can be confusing and outright overwhelming. To get started, we cut through the buzz of the word *passion* and emphasized the importance of seeking deeper contentment and meaning, rather than solely seeking momentary happiness. We introduced a structured approach, reminiscent of something you'd find in corporate strategy, to collect a great amount of information about yourself and distill it into actionable insights.

With that, you have a life strategy to pursue. You have an identity that reflects your values and mission. You have a vision of what you want. You have your *it*, an objective to make your vision come alive. You have concrete goals to bring your vision to fruition.

Now it's about staying the course to pursue the goals you designed—goals that facilitate greater fulfillment and enable you to pursue your passion. While this is your journey, we can't accomplish the most meaningful things in life alone. As you tackle your goals, remember the tips for keeping motivated. Form a community of support and draw on each other for strength. Last but not least, stay honest with yourself.

A Reminder: The Power of the Honest Self

After losing a culinary competition, I recall a chef proudly declaring, "It's still my passion and I'm going to do it." If something remains meaningful, it continues to motivate you to pursue it. There will be great days and less-than-great days, but the good you feel and do will outweigh the negatives if you celebrate who you are and pursue what brings you fulfillment. Trust in who you are and believe in what you want to be.

Your life is your journey. Your honest self is your true self and offers guided direction for your journey. It's up to you to choose the direction you go and what to be in your time. Your honest self provides a natural means of choosing how you spend the time in your life, informing you on which paths to follow and which trails to blaze. Your honest self reminds you: you have your own life to live with unique and valuable gifts to give.

To be your honest self is the greatest form of self-confidence. To be your honest self is the deepest form of self-respect.

Congratulate yourself on the steps you've taken to be confident in who you are, deepen your sense of fulfillment, and grow closer to reaching your goals. You have the tools and the ability, so enjoy the journey ahead.

END NOTES

Preface

1. "100 Best Passion Books of All Time," Book Authority, accessed April 20, 2021, https://bookauthority.org/books/best-passion-books.

Introduction

1. Willie Pietersen, "Why Strategy Is in Trouble," *Ideas and Insights* (blog), *Columbia Business School*, August 15, 2019, https://www8.gsb.columbia.edu/articles/ideas-work/why-strategy-trouble-0.

2. A.G. Lafley and Roger L. Martin, *Playing to Win: How Strategy Really Works* (Boston, MA: Harvard Business Review Press, 2013), 14-15.

Chapter 1

1. *Merriam-Webster*, s.v. "passion (n.)," accessed April 21, 2021, https://www.merriam-webster.com/dictionary/passion.

2. Rachel Weisbrot, "The Metamorphosis of Passion," *Once Upon a Written Word,* February 19, 2018, https://onceuponawrittenword.wordpress.com/2018/02/19/the-metamorphosis-of-passion.

3. Courtney E. Ackerman, "19 Cliché Happiness Quotes & The (Lack Of) Science Behind Them," *Positive Psychology*, January 9, 2000, https://positivepsychology.com/happiness-quotes.

4. Roy F. Baumeister et al., "Some Key Differences between a Happy Life and a Meaningful Life," *The Journal of Positive Psychology* 8, no. 6 (2013), https://doi.org/10.1080/17439760.2013.830764.

5. Scott Barry Kaufman, "Emotionally Extreme Experiences, Not Just 'Positive' or 'Negative' Experiences, Are More Meaningful in Life," *Beautiful Minds* (blog), *Scientific American*, August 21, 2019, https://blogs.scientificamerican.com/beautiful-minds/emotionally-extreme-experiences-not-just-positive-or-negative-experiences-are-more-meaningful-in-life.

6. Wikipedia, s.v. "Amor fati," last modified March 21, 2021, 09:55, https://en.wikipedia.org/wiki/Amor_fati.

7. Saul McLeod, "Maslow's Hierarchy of Needs," *Simple Psychology*, December 29, 2020, https://www.simplypsychology.org/maslow.html.

Chapter 2

1. "Career Change Statistics," Careers Advice Online, accessed August 6, 2021, https://careers-advice-online.com/career-change-statistics.

2. Indeed Editorial Team, "Career Change Report: An Inside Look at Why Workers Shift Gears,". *Indeed*, October 30, 2019, https://www.indeed.com/lead/career-change.

3. Lucy Ash, "Personality Tests: Can They Identify the Real You?" *BBC News*, July 6, 2012, https://www.bbc.com/news/magazine-18723950.

4. "Life Coaches Industry in the US - Market Research Report," IBISWorld, last updated August 30, 2020, https://www.ibisworld.com/united-states/market-research-reports/life-coaches-industry.

5. *Merriam-Webster*, s.v. "obsession (n.)," accessed April 21, 2021, https://www.merriam-webster.com/dictionary/obsession.

6. Mihaly Csikszentmihalyi, *Flow: The Psychology of Optimal Experience* (New York, NY: Harper Perennial Modern Classics, 2008), 9.

Chapter 3

1. *Merriam-Webster*, s.v. "identity (n.)," accessed July 16, 2021, https://www.merriam-webster.com/thesaurus/identity.

Chapter 4

1. Wikipedia, s.v. "James Marcia," last modified July 13, 2021, 03:53, https://en.wikipedia.org/wiki/James_Marcia.

2. "James Marcia," Weebly, accessed September 19, 2021, https://socioemotional.weebly.com/james-marcia.html.

3. Päivi Fadjukoff, Lea Pulkkinen, and Katja Kokko, "Identity Formation in Adulthood: A Longitudinal Study from Age 27 to 50," *Identity* 16, no. 1 (2016): 8-21, https://doi.org/10.1080/15283488.2015.1121820.

4. Seth J. Schwartz, Koen Luyckx, and Vivian L. Vignoles, eds., *Handbook of Identity Theory and Research* (New York, NY: Springer-Verlag, 2011).

5. Rajiv Jhangiani and Hammond Tarry, *Principles of Social Psychology*, 1st international ed. (Victoria, BC: BC Campus, 2014), Chap. 3, Sec. 3. https://opentextbc.ca/socialpsychology/chapter/the-social-self-the-role-of-the-social-situation.

6. "How People Choose 'Career Paths'," *Stanford University News Service*, May 28, 1991, https://news.stanford.edu/pr/91/910528Arc1355.html.

Chapter 5

1. "The Enneagram Personality Test," Truity, accessed August 8, 2021, https://www.truity.com/test/enneagram-personality-test.

2. "Career Personality Profiler," Truity, accessed August 8, 2021, https://www.truity.com/test/career-personality-profiler-test.

3. Live Sonima, "10-Minute Guided Meditation for Self-Compassion," YouTube video, 10:45, April 2, 2015, https://www.youtube.com/watch?v=9TBpGiTrra8.

Chapter 9

1. George B. Bradt, Jayme A. Check, and Jorge E. Pedraza, *The New Leader's 100-Day Action Plan: How to Take Charge, Build Your Team, and Get Immediate Results*, 3rd ed. (Hoboken, NJ: John Wiley & Sons, 2011), 239.

2. The original matrix was first seen during a life coach webinar. While the origin of the original matrix the exercise is based upon is unknown, the creator can contact the author to be credited.

Chapter 10

1. Gretchen Rubin, "The Four Tendencies Quiz," Gretchen Rubin, accessed August 8, 2021, https://quiz.gretchenrubin.com.

2. Niklas Goeke, "The Four Tendencies Summary," *Four Minute Books*, November 2, 2017, https://fourminutebooks.com/the-four-tendencies-summary.

Chapter 11

1. Hugo Alberts and Lucinda Poole, "Goal Visualization," *Positive Psychology*, September 2018, https://positivepsychology.com/wp-content/uploads/2018/09/goal-visualisation-200th-toolkit-tool.pdf.

Chapter 12

1. Courtney E. Ackerman, "18 Self-Esteem Worksheets and Activities for Teens and Adults (+PDFs)," *Positive Psychology*, October 31, 2020, https://positivepsychology.com/self-esteem-worksheets.

2. Carol Dweck, "What Having a 'Growth Mindset' Actually Means," *Harvard Business Review*, January 13, 2016, https://hbr.org/2016/01/what-having-a-growth-mindset-actually-means.

3. Mel Robbins, "The Five Elements of The Five Second Rule," *Mel Robbins Productions*, April 25, 2018, https://melrobbins.com/five-elements-5-second-rule/.

4. Stanford, "1. Introduction to Human Behavioral Biology," YouTube video, 57:14, February 1, 2011, https://www.youtube.com/watch?v=NNnIGh9g6fA.